ideals®
FRIENDSHIP

It is so long a time since we have met,
But friendship spans the deep abyss of time.
We live through yesterdays we shared, and yet
It is so long a time since we have met
To feel the warmth of presence. May we let
This be our mutual hope, our joy sublime:
It is so long a time since we have met,
But friendship spans the deep abyss of time.

Marie Hunter Dawson

Publisher, James A. Kuse

Editor/Ideals, Ralph Luedtke

Managing Editor, Marybeth Owens

Production Manager, Mark Brunner

Photographic Editor, Gerald Koser

Copy Editor, Barbara Nevid

Research Editor, Geraldine Zisk

Art Editor, David Schansberg

ISBN 0-8249-1019-2 350

IDEALS—Vol. 40, No. 4 April MCMLXXXIII IDEALS (ISSN 0019-137X) is published eight times a year,
February, March, April, June, August, September, November, December
by IDEALS PUBLISHING CORPORATION, 11315 Watertown Plank Road, Milwaukee, Wis. 53226
Second class postage paid at Milwaukee, Wisconsin. Copyright © MCMLXXXIII by IDEALS PUBLISHING CORPORATION.
POSTMASTER: Send address changes to Ideals, Post Office Box 2100, Milwaukee, Wis. 53201
All rights reserved. Title IDEALS registered U.S. Patent Office.
Published simultaneously in Canada.

ONE YEAR SUBSCRIPTION—eight consecutive issues as published—$15.95
TWO YEAR SUBSCRIPTION—sixteen consecutive issues as published—$27.95
SINGLE ISSUE—$3.50
Outside U.S.A., add $4.00 per subscription year for postage and handling

The cover and entire contents of IDEALS are fully protected by copyright and must
not be reproduced in any manner whatsoever. Printed and bound in U.S.A.

Welcome Friend

Grace E. Easley

Welcome, friend, how good of you to come!
What pleasant memories your face recalls.
Pull up a chair, and let us sit and talk;
Stay long, for you bring sunlight to these walls.
Welcome, friend, the pot is on the stove;
I'll set another plate beside my own.
Forget your cares; remember two can share
A burden one could never bear alone.

Welcome, friend, I say this from my heart;
You take away the chill of winter days.
I hear the warmth of springtime in your voice,
And after you have gone, the wonder stays.
The fact that you have cared enough to come
Means more to me than words can ever say.
The light of friendship glows within your eyes,
And that is why I welcome you today.

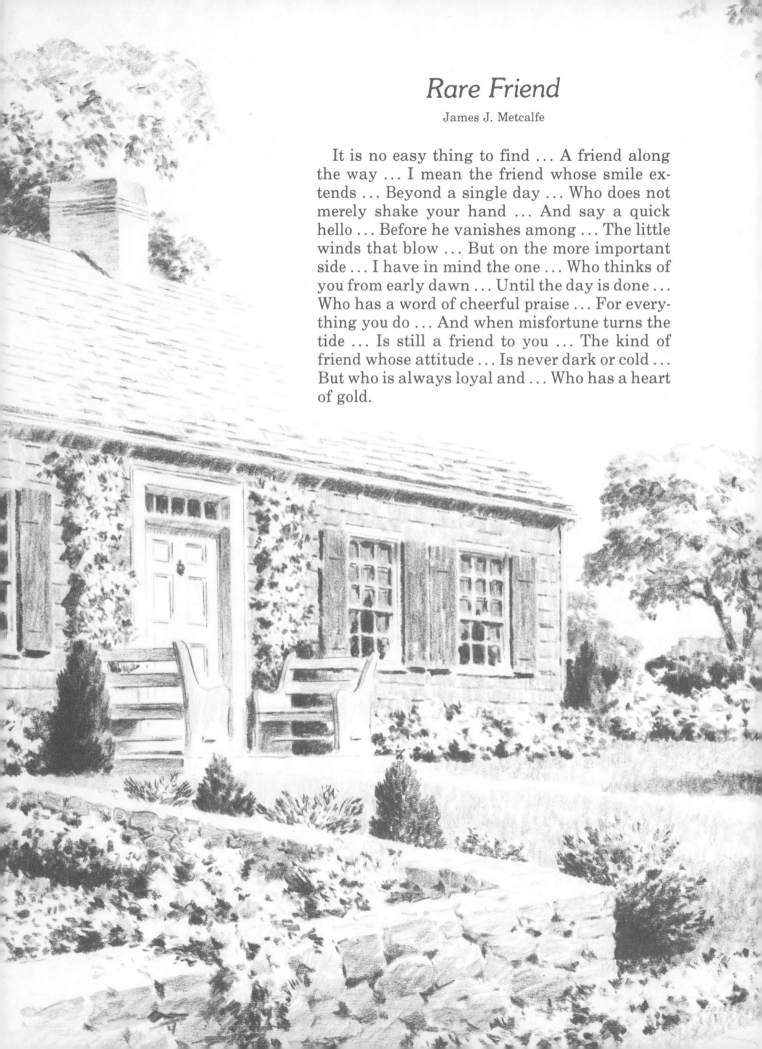

Rare Friend

James J. Metcalfe

It is no easy thing to find ... A friend along the way ... I mean the friend whose smile extends ... Beyond a single day ... Who does not merely shake your hand ... And say a quick hello ... Before he vanishes among ... The little winds that blow ... But on the more important side ... I have in mind the one ... Who thinks of you from early dawn ... Until the day is done ... Who has a word of cheerful praise ... For everything you do ... And when misfortune turns the tide ... Is still a friend to you ... The kind of friend whose attitude ... Is never dark or cold ... But who is always loyal and ... Who has a heart of gold.

Friendly Flowers

Owen Gaddis

I love the little flowers
   in the garden that I tend.
Because to me each one of them
   is like a special friend.
In fact, when I am planting them,
   I name them, one and all,
According to the titles of the
   faces I recall.

I give each one the best of care
   to help their petals grow,
The same as I would serve the
   needs of every friend I know.
My little flowers represent the
   folks who favor me
With kindness and companionship
   and gentle sympathy.

They are the understanding souls
   who whisper to my heart
The sentiments with which no friends
   could ever grow apart.

The Carnation

Gail Brook Burket

Carnations' spicy fragrance fills
My mind with glamorous old tales
Of life in Greece long years ago—
Young shepherds piping in the vales,
White temples crowning highest hills,
Gold-laden ships with purple sails,
And splendid feasts where heroes wore
Carnation crowns about their brow.
"The coronation flower" was loved
By people then, as it is now.

Great marble temples toppled down
And crumbled into heaps of stone.
The piping shepherds lost their youth,
And ships, on which the sun once shone,
No longer danced across the sea.
Of all things then, a flower, alone,
Has not grown old through countless years.
Today carnation buds unfold
With same fresh tints and spicy scent
As in the Grecian Age of Gold.

Picture opposite
Gerald Koser

Henry van Dyke

Henry van Dyke—clergyman, lecturer, writer, diplomat—was born in Germantown, Pennsylvania, in 1852. In his early thirties, he served as pastor of Brick Presbyterian Church in New York City where his preaching ability soon won him national recognition. His poetry and short stories were widely published.

In 1900 he became a professor of English literature at Princeton University. Later, President Wilson appointed him to the office of minister to the Netherlands and Luxembourg. He served as navy chaplain in World War I, with the rank of lieutenant commander.

Dr. van Dyke was truly a man of many talents. In his poetry and short stories, he left us a legacy of literary art filled with beautiful thoughts and high ideals.

Finding a Friend

A theory of friendship is a good thing for you to have. It is precious. It elevates and cheers your mind. But presently, as you go on your way through the world, you find a friend: one who comes close to you in that mysterious contact of personalities which is the most wonderful thing in the world; one who knows you, cares for you, loves you, gives you the sacred gifts of fellowship and help. Trouble befalls you. Your friend stands by you, strengthens you, counsels you, helps you to fight your way out of that which is conquerable and to endure patiently that which is inevitable.

Rendezvous

I count that friendship little worth
Which has not many things untold,
Great longings that no words can hold,
And passion-secrets waiting birth.

Along the slender wires of speech
Some message from the heart is sent;
But who can tell the whole that's meant?
Our dearest thoughts are out of reach.

I have not seen thee, though mine eyes
Hold now the image of thy face;
In vain, through form, I strive to trace
The soul I love, that deeper lies.

A thousand accidents control
Our meeting here. Clasp hand in hand,
And swear to meet me in that land
Where friends hold converse soul to soul.

Time

Time is
Too slow for those who wait,
Too swift for those who fear,
Too long for those who grieve,
Too short for those who rejoice;
but for those who love,
Time is not.

Friendly Talk

But after all, the very best thing in good talk, and the thing that helps it most, is friendship. How it dissolves the barriers that divide us and loosens all constraint and diffuses itself like some fine old cordial through all the veins of life—this feeling that we understand and trust each other and wish each other heartily well! Everything into which it really comes is good. It transforms letter-writing from a task into a pleasure. It makes music a thousand times more sweet. The people who play and sing not at us, but to us—how delightful it is to listen to them! Yes, there is a talkability that can express itself even without words. There is an exchange of thought and feeling which is happy alike in speech and in silence. It is quietness pervaded with friendship.

A Skylark Singing

The first time that I ever heard the skylark was on the great plain of Salisbury. Sheep were feeding, and shepherds were watching nearby. From the contentment of her lowly nest in the grass, the songstress rose on quivering wings, pouring out a perfect flood of joy. With infinite courage, the feathered atom breasted the spaces of the sky as if her music lifted her irresistibly upward. With sublime confidence, she passed out of sight into the azure, but not out of hearing; for her cheerful voice fell yet more sweetly through the distance as if it were saying, "Forever, forever!"

Life-Giving Love

Surely there is nothing else in all the world so life-giving as the knowledge that we are loved. Even in our human relationships when this knowledge comes to us, it lifts us out of the dust and thrills us with vital power. How many a heart has been revived and emancipated, enlarged and ennobled by knowing that somewhere in the world there was another heart moving toward it in the tenderness and glory of love.

A Mile with Me

Oh, who will walk a mile with me
  Along life's merry way?
A comrade blithe and full of glee
Who dares to laugh out loud and free,
And let his frolic fancy play
Like a happy child, through the flowers gay
That fill the field and fringe the way
  Where he walks a mile with me.

And who will walk a mile with me
  Along life's weary way?
A friend whose heart has eyes to see
The stars shine out o'er the darkening lea,
And the quiet rest at the end of the day,
A friend who knows and dares to say
The brave, sweet words that cheer the way
  Where he walks a mile with me.

With such a comrade, such a friend,
I fain would walk till journey's end
Through summer sunshine, winter rain,
And then—farewell, we shall meet again!

Contrasts

If all the skies were sunshine,
  Our faces would be fain
To feel once more upon them
  The cooling splash of rain.

If all the world were music,
  Our hearts would often long
For one sweet strain of silence
  To break the endless song.

If life were always merry,
  Our souls would seek relief
And rest from weary laughter
  In the quiet arms of grief.

Fairy Slippers

Caroline Henning Bair

The fairies must have danced last night,
For in the misty dawn,
Some little lady's slippers gleamed
Upon the grassy lawn.

They were a golden-yellow hue,
The kind that fairies wear.
So beautiful and fragilelike,
I sought to leave them there.

And then to my surprise, I saw
Each had a slim green rod
That held it gracefully and firm
Above the cool, moist sod.

Lady's Slippers

Annie Laurie

Lovely, dainty lady's slippers—lavender and lace,
Growing through the mosses in this shady place,
I've been searching for you in all the hidden nooks,
Expecting to find you there or by the moss-fringed brooks.

I'd just about decided that I'd dreamed you long ago
When as a child, lady's slipper hunting I would go;
For I've not seen your likeness in more than forty years
Except as your image in my memory appears.

Picture opposite
LADY'S SLIPPERS,
Door County, Wisconsin
Ken Dequaine

The House by the Side of the Road

Sam Walter Foss

There are hermit souls that live withdrawn
In the place of their self-content;
There are souls like stars, that dwell apart,
In a fellowless firmament;
There are pioneer souls that blaze their paths
Where highways never ran—
But let me live by the side of the road
And be a friend to man.

Let me live in a house by the side of the road,
Where the race of men go by—
The men who are good and the men who are bad,
As good and as bad as I.
I would not sit in the scorner's seat,
Or hurl the cynic's ban.
Let me live in a house by the side of the road
And be a friend to man.

I see from my house by the side of the road,
By the side of the highway of life,
The men who press with the ardor of hope,
The men who are faint with the strife.
But I turn not away from their smiles nor their tears,
Both parts of an infinite plan—
Let me live in a house by the side of the road
And be a friend to man.

I know there are brook-gladdened meadows ahead,
And mountains of wearisome height;
That the road passes on through the long afternoon
And stretches away to the night.
But still I rejoice when the travelers rejoice,
And weep with the strangers that moan,
Nor live in my house by the side of the road
Like a man who dwells alone.

Let me live in my house by the side of the road;
It's here the race of men go by.
They are good, they are bad, they are weak, they are strong,
Wise, foolish—so am I;
Then why should I sit in the scorner's seat,
Or hurl the cynic's ban?
Let me live in my house by the side of the road
And be a friend to man.

The Garden Gate

Betty G. Ahearn

There's something about a garden
 gate
That invites the soul to meditate,
To enter a garden beyond a wall—
Where living things have heard
 God's call,
Where one can sit and marvel at
 views
Of nature painted in brilliant
 hues—
To listen to birds and whispering
 sounds
And know creative love abounds,
At last to feel the kiss of the sun
For pleasant dreams when the day
 is done.

Good Friends

Freda V. Fisher

Good friends are like a garden
 with blossoms sweet and rare;
They need our sure companionship;
 they need our constant care.

The blooms of early springtime
 oft linger through the year,
And friendships formed in early youth
 remain so very dear.

But blossoms of the winter months,
 surviving through the storms,
Like friends we meet in later years,
 light a fire within that warms.

Picture opposite
Fred Sieb

My Guest

Alice Leedy Mason

Dear little friend
In black cap and vest,
Fashion declares you
Tastefully dressed.
I'm truly charmed
That you are my guest.

Your jet set flies
All over the land,
Dines of cuisines
Exotic and grand,
But you prefer seeds
I hold in my hand.

A Friend

Robert Freeman Bound

Then it's up and away
By a sun-dappled bay
Where the ribbon road unwinds;
For the month is June,
And my world's a-bloom.
Farewell to the tie that binds!

I'm not in search of a bluebird
In some visionary land,
For, you see, there's one on my shoulder
That sings and feeds from my hand!

Picture opposite
CHICKADEE
Fred Sieh

The Country Storekeeper

Ruth B. Field

The keeper of the country store
  has a most enchanting place
That smells of coffee, cheese, and spices,
  and with an easy grace
He measures yards of calico,
  puts up beans or fish,
Penny candy, magic yeast—
  most anything you wish.

He visits with his neighbors
  and knows everyone by name;
At times, by the potbellied stove,
  will play a checker game.
The cracker barrel is standing near,
  fresh eggs and butter, too,
Maple sugar—and he'll spin
  a country tale or two.

Not only can we find in here
  real treasure on the shelves,
But in this homey atmosphere,
  we garner for ourselves
Bits of wisdom, laughter, peace,
  which folks need more and more,
And it doesn't cost us even a cent
  in the country store.

The Old Hometown

P. F. Freeman

When it's near the close of day
  And months into years have grown,
There comes a feeling of delight
  As I think of the folks at home.
The old hometown has changed a lot,
  But one fact remains the same—
Through the years, no matter what,
  They never changed the name.

A creaking pump stands in the square,
  Not good as it used to be,
And there's yet a wooden bench
  Beneath the old elm tree.
Each year they hold a county fair,
  Its displays have gained renown,
And a weekly paper lets me know
  What's happening in the old hometown.

I often think of an iron stove
  Down at the village store
And how the menfolks, for a chat,
  Would gather by the score.
When the hours are so lonely
  And there's not a soul around,
It's then I think of all the folks
  Back in the old hometown.

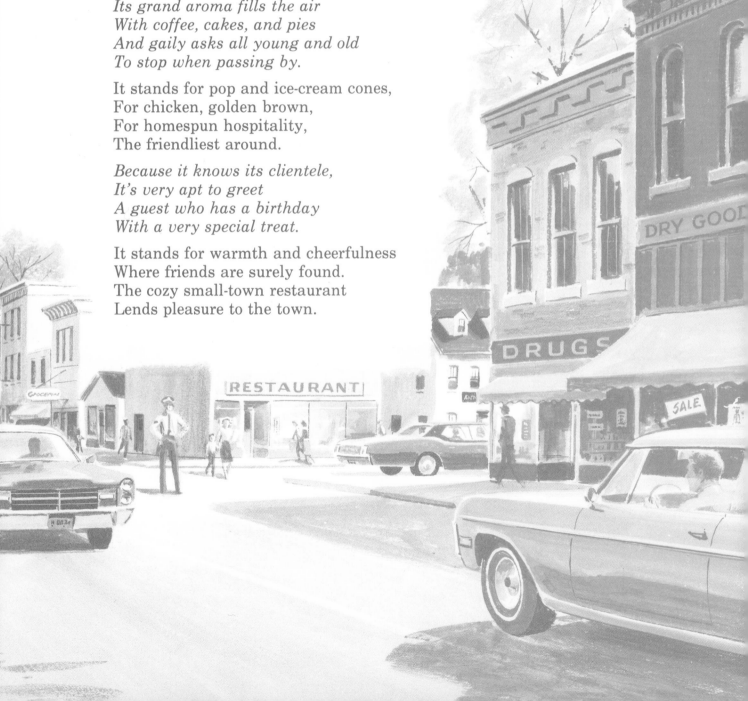

Small Town Café

Craig E. Sathoff

The friendly small-town restaurant
Is busy as can be.
It serves as meeting place for all
And town directory.

Its grand aroma fills the air
With coffee, cakes, and pies
And gaily asks all young and old
To stop when passing by.

It stands for pop and ice-cream cones,
For chicken, golden brown,
For homespun hospitality,
The friendliest around.

Because it knows its clientele,
It's very apt to greet
A guest who has a birthday
With a very special treat.

It stands for warmth and cheerfulness
Where friends are surely found.
The cozy small-town restaurant
Lends pleasure to the town.

Friendship Village

Fred Toothaker

'Twas a friendly little village
    in a scenic countryside,
Where the folks all knew each other
    and where kindness was their guide.
When a neighbor had some problem,
    there was willing help at hand
Of the kind that only neighbors
    in this village understand.
All the children play together
    in the best of harmony,
Freely sharing all their playthings
    and their pleasures peacefully.
All around that pleasant village
    was a friendly atmosphere
Giving visitors the feeling
    of "glad to have you here."
Even though you were a stranger,
    folks would greet you with a smile
Of the kind that offered welcome
    if you'd like to stay awhile.

The making of friends who are real friends is the
best token we have of a man's success in life.

Edward Everett Hale

Friendship is something you consider for a moment,
but cherish for an eternity.

Tim Traynor

Painting opposite
WATERMILL AT GILLINGHAM
John Constable

Overleaf
CEDARBURG, WISCONSIN
Gerald Koser

The Things I Prize

Garnett Ann Schultz

The fresh smell of the summer breeze,
The crimson of the skies,
The golden glint of morning's sun—
These are the things I prize.
The fragrance of a budding rose
With petals bright and wet,
The picture that I treasure most
Is God's own sweet sunset.

Just simple little untold joys
And love from someone dear,
I only want a heart content,
A mind that's free from fear.
I prize the wishes I can make,
The dreams that I can dream,
The pictures that my mind can paint,
So much I've never seen.

I wouldn't trade one precious note
Those little birds can sing.
I'll ever praise our God above
For every little thing.
The things I prize are oh, so small,
So simple in their way—
A friendly smile because I'm loved
And needed every day.

I wouldn't want the greatest wealth;
I'd rather have a friend.
My heart can only know the peace
That love and kindness lend.
I have the world within my grasp
With pleasant sweet surprise,
And joys that life has given me—
These are the things I prize.

CONCERNING FRIENDSHIP

Harry B. Hawes

All that can be expected of any man is to make the best use of the things that are within his power.

Only the contented man is rich, so we must look for the things that bring contentment.

And first of these is to find a friend; and if you find two friends, you are indeed a lucky man; and if you find three friends, real friends, then you are a rich and powerful man.

In prosperity it is easy to find a friend, but in adversity it is most difficult of all things.

No matter how small a man's means may be, if he gives of what he has to his friend it is the same as if it were a great amount.

A man's pleasures are insured by sharing them with a friend, and his griefs are reduced by securing the sympathy of a friend.

The counsel of a friend is the best counsel because it will be true advice; for when received from a mere acquaintance, it may be so filled with flattery that its value will be destroyed; and faithful and true counsel rarely comes excepting from the true friend.

It is said that in youth we have visions and in old age, dreams, and the vision and the dream may give us an ideal of perfection; but experience and large contact with men compel us to accept the man who measures in his virtues only the substantial average.

If we view a man as a whole and find him good as a friend, we must not be diverted from the happy average—the everyday, human average—by using a magnifying glass upon his faults or frailties.

We must, in order to have and hold a friend, accept him as he is, demanding but one thing in return for our affection—his fidelity.

CICERO'S OPINION

Translated by W. Melmoth

I can only exhort you to look on friendship as the most valuable of all human possessions, no other being equally suited to the moral nature of man, or so applicable to every state and circumstance, whether of prosperity or adversity, in which he can possibly be placed. But at the same time I lay it down as a fundamental axiom that "true friendship can only subsist between those who are animated by the strictest principles of honor and virtue. . . ."

But what still farther evinces the strength and efficacy of friendship above all the numberless other social tendencies of the human heart is that, instead of wasting its force upon a multiplicity of divided objects, its whole energy is exerted for the benefit of only two or three persons at the utmost.

Friendship may be shortly defined, "a perfect conformity of opinions upon all religious and civil subjects, united with the highest degree of mutual esteem and affection"; and yet from these simple circumstances results the most desirable blessing (virtue alone excepted) that the gods have bestowed on mankind.

It is virtue, yes, let me repeat it again, it is virtue alone that can give birth, strength, and permanency to friendship. For virtue is a uniform and steady principle ever acting consistently with itself. They whose souls are warmed by its generous flames not only improve their common ardor by communication, but naturally kindle into that pure affection of the heart towards each other which is distinguished by the name of amity and is wholly unmixed with every kind and degree of selfish considerations. Since man holds all his possessions by a very precarious and uncertain tenure, we should endeavor, as our old friends drop off, to repair their loss by new acquisitions, lest one should be so unhappy as to stand in his old age a solitary, unconnected individual, bereaved of every person whom he loves and by whom he is loved. For without a proper and particular object upon which to exercise the kind and benevolent affections, life is destitute of every enjoyment that can render it justly desirable.

Seaside Thoughts

Vera Ramsdell Hardman

Friendship is like the rolling sea,
And each wave always brings
A thought of friends I cherish most,
And my heart fairly sings.

The white tops riding far at sea
Remind me of those friends
Where, though the miles stretch far between,
Our friendship never ends.

And as the tide breaks on the shore,
I watch it ebb and flow
As memories of friends held dear
So fondly come and go.

Then as I look far out to sea
Where water meets the skies,
Just as heaven and earth are joined,
So friendship, two hearts ties.

Picture opposite
NUBBLE LIGHTHOUSE, MAINE
Monserrate J. Schwartz

Norman Rockwell

Little Spooners

The earth is changing wardrobes,
The time is early spring,
The daffodils are popping out,
And birds begin to sing.
The days are getting longer,
Foul weather's turned to fair,
The nights are feeling warmer,
And sweet fragrance fills the air.
The April moon is hanging
Like a great balloon above,
And every young man's fancy
Has turned to thoughts of love.

And at this moment everywhere,
Life's problems turn to bliss
As each shy lad looks at the moon
With his arm around his miss.
And without a poem from the pen
Of any famous poet
And without a story from the men
Who speak for all to know it
And without a song from writers
Who write the tunes for crooners,
This evening of unspoken love
Belongs to *Little Spooners*.

Norman Rockwell's "Little Spooners"

Little Spooners or *First Love* appeared on the cover of the *Saturday Evening Post* on April, 24, 1926, and instantly became one of the most popular paintings ever created by the great American artist and illustrator Norman Rockwell. Today, over five decades later, it is still one of the most sought-after illustrations and has been re-created on calendars, on greeting cards, on china plates, in books, and as porcelain figurines.

From the time Norman Rockwell was a young boy in New York City, he loved to sketch children and dogs. On Sunday afternoons, the Rockwell family would take a trolley-car ride to the park, and he would spend hours drawing kids fishing, swimming, and playing ball. As the years passed and his fame grew, he never deviated from his admiration of children. He loved their beauty, their unpretentiousness, and their boundless energy, and this love showed in his work.

And dogs—Rockwell soon found out that the public certainly couldn't resist dogs, and he capitalized on this fact. The Rockwell family always had a dog, so a model was always available. Occasionally, a local stray was also a suitable model.

Norman Rockwell began his career with the *Saturday Evening Post* in March, 1916. Reluctantly heeding the advice of friends, he journeyed to Philadelphia with four of his paintings. There he met with George Horace Lorimer, the Curtis Publishing Company's editor, who was instantly impressed with the young artist. Mr. Rockwell left the meeting a short time later with $150 in his pocket, and Mr. Lorimer had two paintings and the beginning of an American legend. *Little Spooners* was the eighty-sixth cover that Mr. Rockwell painted for the magazine.

Rockwell was able to live comfortably in New Rochelle, New York, as a result of the success of his work. He took several trips to Europe with the hope of enriching himself and finding new interests and subject matter. No matter how he tried, however, he kept coming back to the things he knew, loved, and painted best—little boys, little girls, and little dogs.

As the art director for the Boy Scouts of America, he had an opportunity to paint more pictures featuring boys. He also illustrated many books, magazines, and advertisements.

The association between the Curtis Publishing Company and Norman Rockwell lasted almost sixty years. He painted 324 magazine covers for the *Saturday Evening Post,* but no cover was more recognized, more loved and more remembered than *Little Spooners*.

Dr. Donald R. Stoltz, President
The Norman Rockwell Museum
Philadelphia, Pennsylvania

Painting opposite
LITTLE SPOONERS
Norman Rockwell

Intelligent Cat

Grace Bacon Holway

A rush and a dash and a scamper,
A warm, nestling armful of fur,
Our brief game of tag—being over—
Gave place to the tenderest purr.

He measures a yard in the morning
When stretched in a sweet, dreamless sleep,
The rich tawny fur, soft as velvet,
Showing broad, even stripes, dark and deep.

He lies on my lap in the sunshine;
I rock him to sleep on my arm;
I feel all the pleasure of loving
And striving to shield him from harm.

He runs up the tree to my window
To tap with his paw on the pane
And plead, in his sweet coaxing language,
For comfort and shelter again.

Each movement of gentle contentment,
Replete with luxurious grace,
Proclaims him at once and forever
The king of the feline race.

Picture opposite
SHORT-HAIRED TABBY KITTENS
Colour Library Intl. (USA) Limited

Friendship

Irene Y. Packard

Friendship's a gift, priceless and rare,
　So gentle, so tender, and true;
Strong as a bond holding earth to the sun,
　Yet light as the thistledown, too!

Holding, enfolding in thoughtful embrace,
　Yet leaving one free as the air;
Asking no thing in return for its gift—
　When needed, it always is there.

Time neither changes nor alters its glow;
　It brightens a long weary road.
Knowing a friend is there by your side
　Can lighten the heaviest load.

And as the sun peeks past the dark clouds
　When sorrow and grief are at end,
Joys that there are, are sweeter by far
　If shared by a dear thoughtful friend.

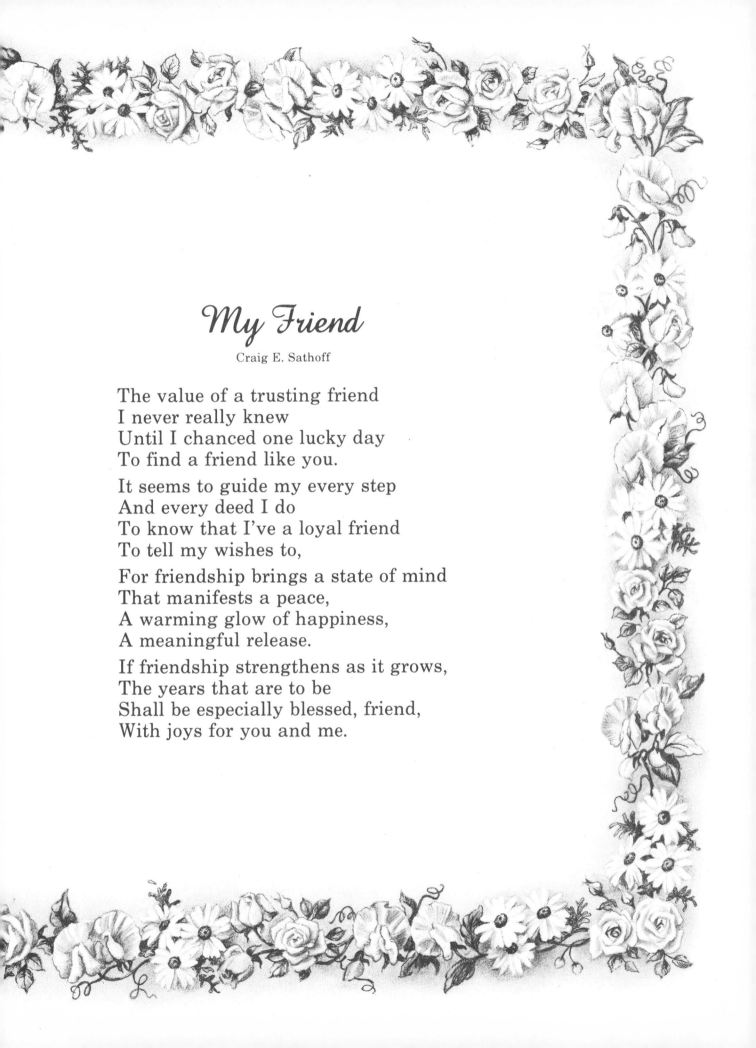

My Friend

Craig E. Sathoff

The value of a trusting friend
I never really knew
Until I chanced one lucky day
To find a friend like you.

It seems to guide my every step
And every deed I do
To know that I've a loyal friend
To tell my wishes to,

For friendship brings a state of mind
That manifests a peace,
A warming glow of happiness,
A meaningful release.

If friendship strengthens as it grows,
The years that are to be
Shall be especially blessed, friend,
With joys for you and me.

The Eagle

James Gates Percival

Bird of the broad and sweeping wing,
Thy home is high in heaven
Where the wide storms their banners fling
And the tempest-clouds are driven.
Thy throne is on the mountaintop;
Thy fields, the boundless air;
And hoary peaks that proudly prop
The skies, thy dwellings are.

Thou art perched aloft on the beetling crag,
And the waves are white below,
And on, with a haste that cannot lag,
They rush in an endless flow.
Again thou hast plumed thy wing for flight
To lands beyond the sea,
And away, like a spirit wreathed in light,
Thou hurriest, wild and free.

Lord of the boundless realm of air,
In thy imperial name
The hearts of the bold and ardent dare
The dangerous path of fame.
Beneath the shade of thy golden wings,
The Roman legions bore,
From the river of Egypt's cloudy springs,
Their pride to the polar shore.

For thee they fought; for thee they fell,
And their oath on thee was laid;
To thee the clarions raised their swell,
And the dying warrior prayed.
Thou wert, through an age of death and fears,
The image of pride and power
Till the gathered rage of a thousand years
Burst forth in one awful hour.

And then, a deluge of wrath it came,
And the nations shook with dread,
And it swept the earth till its fields were flame
And piled with the mingled dead.
Kings were rolled in the wasteful flood
With the low and crouching slave,
And together lay in a shroud of blood,
The coward and the brave.

And where was then thy fearless flight?
O'er the dark and mysterious sea
To the land that caught the setting light,
The cradle of liberty.
There, on the silent and lonely shore,
For ages I watched alone,
And the world, in its darkness, asked no more
Where the glorious bird had flown.

But then, came a bold and hardy few,
And they breasted the unknown wave;
I saw from far the wandering crew,
And I knew they were high and brave.
I wheeled around the welcome bark
As it sought the desolate shore,
And up to heaven, like a joyous lark,
My quivering pinions bore.

And now, that bold and hardy few
Are a nation wide and strong;
And danger and doubt I have led them through,
And they worship me in song;
And over their bright and glancing arms,
On field and lake and sea,
With an eye that fires and a spell that charms,
I guide them to victory!

Painting opposite
BALD EAGLE
Harry J. Moeller

BETWEEN BOOK ENDS

In my bookcase they stand and stand,
These friends of mine that understand,
Bound in wisdom that is profound
From pages old the world around.

Tattered, yellowed with pages torn,
They are my friends, all ages worn;
Some are soiled and by tears are marked,
These old, old friends, each patriarch.

They are my friends; they serve me well
And often in my search will tell
Some little thing I want to know
To guide me on, to help me grow.

Gertrude Rudberg

My life is a chronicle of friendship. My friends—
all those about me—create my world anew each
day. Without their loving care all the courage I
could summon would not suffice to keep my
heart strong for life. But, like Stevenson, I know it
is better to do things than to imagine them.

Helen Keller

It is pleasant to have people love you even when
they don't know you. But of more value is the
love of the friend who has found you out and still
loves you.

Author Unknown

He drew a circle that shut me out—
Heretic, rebel, a thing to flout.
But Love and I had the wit to win;
We drew a circle that took him in!

Edwin Markham

Walk on a rainbow trail, walk on a trail of song,
and all about you will be beauty. There is a way
out of every dark mist, over a rainbow trail.

Navajo Song

The things that the flag stands for were created by the experiences of a great people. Everything that it stands for was written by their lives. The flag is the embodiment, not of sentiment, but of history. It represents the experiences made by men and women, the experiences of those who do and live under that flag.

Woodrow Wilson

Greater love hath no man than this, that a man lay down his life for his friends.

John 15:13

The grass flames up on the hillsides like a spring fire as if the earth sent forth an inward heat to greet the returning sun; not yellow but green is the color of its flame; the symbol of perpetual youth, the grass-blade, like a long green ribbon, streams from the sod into the summer.

Henry David Thoreau

Seek the silent woodland
Where no sound of wheels is heard
And nothing breaks the stillness
Save the singing of a bird.

Nature tells her secrets
Not to those who hurry by,
But to those who walk
With happy heart and seeing eye.

Patience Strong

Elysium is as far as to
The very nearest room,
If in that room a friend awaits
Felicity or doom.

Emily Dickinson

The most precious things in life are near at hand, without money and without price. Each of you has the whole wealth of the universe at your very door. All that I ever had, or still have, may be yours by stretching forth your hand and taking it.

John Burroughs

And what is so rare as a day in June!
Then, if ever, come perfect days;
Then Heaven tries the earth if it be in tune,
And over it softly her warm ear lays.
Whether we look or whether we listen,
We hear life murmur or see it glisten;
Every clod feels a stir of might,
An instinct within it that reaches and towers,
And groping blindly above it for light,
Climbs to a soul in grass and flowers.

James Russell Lowell

H.MOELLER.

My Father

Grace V. Watkins

My father used to take me by the hand
And lead me out into a summer wood
And teach my heart to love and understand
The wind, the sun and shadow and the good
Brown carpet of the leaves from other years.
And he would tell me, "See the birds that bless
The woodland kingdom; oftentimes their ears
Hear loveliness we cannot even guess."
My father was a man of simple speech;
Though he possessed no eloquence of tongue,
He taught me secrets so that I could reach
Uplands of wonderment while I was young,
And looking through his eyes, I learned to see
The lighted foothills of eternity.

Painting opposite
WOOD DUCKS
Harry J. Moeller

The Art of Edwina

Early in the twenties, Edwina Dumm created her memorable comic strip, *Tippie and "Cap" Stubbs*. First published in New York City, its popularity grew until it was featured in newspapers throughout the country.

Tippie and "Cap" Stubbs was one of those "funnies" that really made you laugh. The story centered around the humorous antics of a young boy named Cap Stubbs, his dog Tippie, and his stern but fun-loving Gran'ma.

Like a Norman Rockwell painting, Edwina's characters were sure to wrap up a difficult situation in a way that left you smiling.

ALEC the GREAT

Long friendships often Terminate, When seeds of envy Germinate.

How hard it is to tell a friend He, too, Has faults as bad as those he finds In you.

I envy my friends When a problem I face, For they are so sure What they'd do in my place.

When two people Choose to vary, Who can say which One's contrary?

After All He Did For Her

Tippie and "Cap" Stubbs

by EDWINA

He Waits for Me

Craig E. Sathoff

He waits for me most patiently
Beside the front-lawn gate
With just a bit of anxiousness
If I should come home late.

Of course, my family shows delight
To see me home again,
But he who waits with wagging tail
Is first to see me in.

His eyes a-sparkle with his joy,
He seems to want to say
That he has missed me very much
While I have been away.

I pat his fluffy little head
Because I know it's true
That I adore his friendly ways,
And I have missed him, too.

Picture opposite
WELSH CORGIS
Freelance Photographers Guild,
New York

THE STORY OF "TAPS"

Of all the bugle calls used in the United States armed service, none is more popular or better known than "Taps." Probably not one American in twenty has heard of how this famous call was first blown.

It happened in Virginia in July, 1862. After seven days of bitter fighting before Richmond, the North's Army of the Potomac lay encamped at Harrison's Landing on the James River. Vacant places in the ranks were a sharp reminder of the heavy losses that had been suffered, and to officers and men alike, there now came a sobering realization of what a terrible toll the War Between the States was sure to take before it was over.

Up and down the long, winding valley rose the bugle calls, echoing to the distant hills. The rhythm of camp life was punctuated by these soaring notes. If it had not been for tents and uniforms, the setting would have suited a summer idyll.

Now, with time heavy on his hands, the thoughts of more than one soldier turned to home and loved ones in the North. As nostalgia rested heavily on the troops, the close of each day found many men in a mood not untouched with sadness.

Some of this feeling must have crept into the consciousness of General Daniel Butterfield. A brave commander, he was also an expert musician, with ears keenly attuned to harmony. While homesickness pervaded the Army and the nights were filled with tender retrospection, he took a sudden dislike to the discordant "Lights Out" call, which had been handed down from the early days of West Point.

All by himself, he began to turn over in his mind a combination of notes that would express the peacefulness of a great camp after nightfall—soldiers sleeping, sentries keeping watch under the stars, rest after labor. The scene must have inspired the musical phrases of "Taps."

When General Butterfield was satisfied with his musical combination, he sent for his brigade bugler, Oliver W. Norton.

Whistling the notes over and over, he taught them to the young musician. Whenever Norton made a mistake, General Butterfield would correct him, and the result was that in a short time the bugler was able to blow "Taps" perfectly. In order to preserve the call, the general copied down the notes with a pencil on the back of an old envelope.

That same night General Butterfield's brigade was the first to hear the lingering refrain. Its music carried up and down the valley, and the wistful, haunting notes struck a responsive chord with thousands of other listeners.

The next morning General Butterfield was besieged by the buglers of other camps. "Taps" had caught their fancy, and they were curious about it. They wanted to know its origin, its meaning and even asked for a copy of the music. All were given permission to use it.

Whenever the new "Lights Out" was blown among Union forces after that, it excited immediate interest. The music lingered in the memory, and every soldier came to love it. It passed from corps to corps until, at last, by general orders, it was substituted for the old "Lights Out" call and was officially printed in the army regulations.

Since that time, as everybody knows, "Taps" has become an American tradition. It is used for the military burial service by the veterans of all wars. That use has undoubtedly given it the most poignant associations. It moves listeners as no other bugle call can, and at the first notes a hush will fall over the noisiest crowd.

Life was certainly kind to the call's composer. At the close of the war, General Butterfield entered business in New York, where, by reason of his great organizing ability, he was frequently called upon to take charge of public parades and exhibitions. When he finally retired, it was to a home at Cold Spring, New York, where, just across the Hudson, he could hear the notes of his beloved "Taps" sounded every evening by the bugler at West Point.

George Daniels

Taps

Arfa Nottingham Chappius

There will be a great encampment
In the land of clouds today,
A mingling and a merging
Of the men in blue and gray.
Though on earth they are disbanding,
They are very close and near,
For these brave and honored soldiers
Show no sorrow, shed no tear.
They have lived a life of glory;
History pins their medals high.
Listen to the thunder rolling;
They are marching in the sky!

Origin of Flag Day

It was Sunday, June 14. The year was 1885. The people of Waubeka, Wisconsin, a little farming town nestled near the headwaters of the Milwaukee River, were invited to a birthday party that would bring them national acclaim. The party was the brainchild of Bernard J. Cigrand, young schoolmaster of the Stony Hill School. Cigrand had asked his pupils to observe a Flag Birthday in honor of the 108-year-old American flag.

For months the children of Waubeka had been rehearsing their part in the celebration. The little stone schoolhouse was patriotically decorated with dozens of flags. Many were homemade. One small flag was placed in a tall, thin bottle on the schoolmaster's desk. Refreshments included a large cake, baked by one of the mothers, and cool, refreshing lemonade for everyone.

The program began. Small girls dressed in their best white dresses recited short pieces. The older children recited poems and told stories about the American flag. The story was told of Francis Scott Key who wrote a poem about the flag and the brave men who kept it flying during the War of 1812. The name of that poem was "The Star-Spangled Banner." After everyone joined in a pledge of loyalty to the flag, the party ended.

Cigrand never let the idea of a special day to honor the flag die. He made speeches and wrote articles reminding Americans of the need to honor their flag. Because of his efforts, he was known as the father of Flag Day.

There were others who helped keep the idea alive. Every year, New York schools were requested to have special programs on June 14. Even the mayor of Philadelphia ordered flags flown on all civic buildings in honor of the date. Later, in 1916, President Woodrow Wilson officially proclaimed June 14 to be Flag Day.

Little did the people who attended that long-ago Flag Birthday know that they were originating a lasting tribute to our flag—a tribute which resulted from the determined efforts of the young schoolmaster of Stony Hill School.

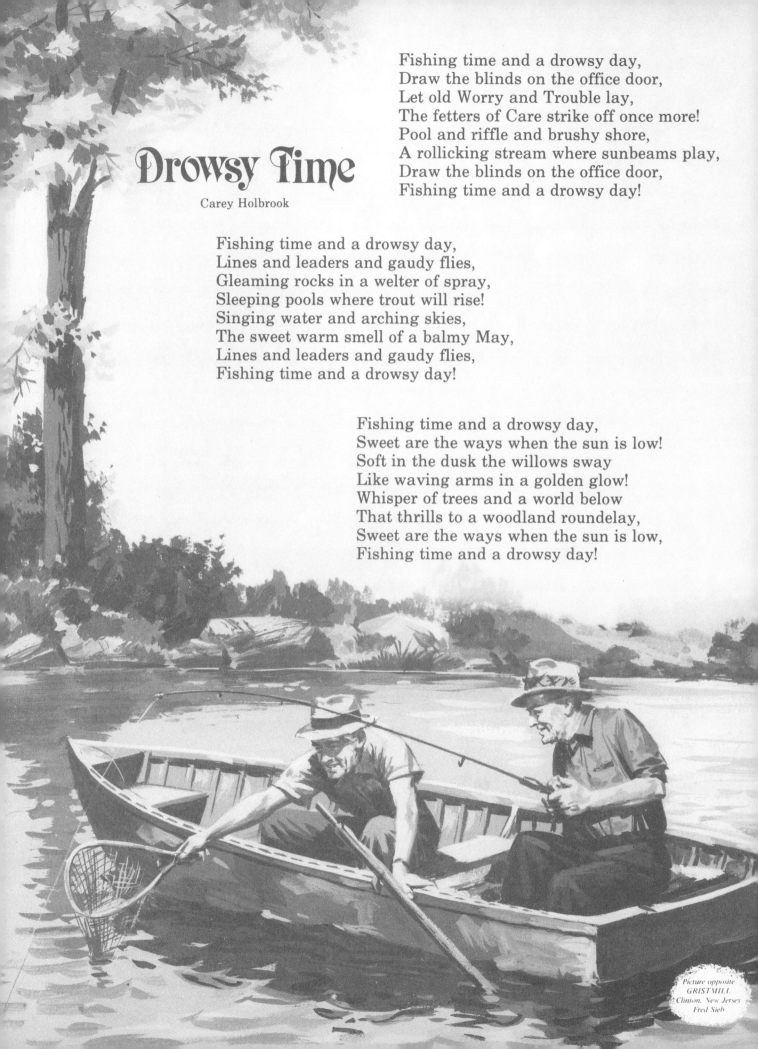

Drowsy Time

Carey Holbrook

Fishing time and a drowsy day,
Draw the blinds on the office door,
Let old Worry and Trouble lay,
The fetters of Care strike off once more!
Pool and riffle and brushy shore,
A rollicking stream where sunbeams play,
Draw the blinds on the office door,
Fishing time and a drowsy day!

Fishing time and a drowsy day,
Lines and leaders and gaudy flies,
Gleaming rocks in a welter of spray,
Sleeping pools where trout will rise!
Singing water and arching skies,
The sweet warm smell of a balmy May,
Lines and leaders and gaudy flies,
Fishing time and a drowsy day!

Fishing time and a drowsy day,
Sweet are the ways when the sun is low!
Soft in the dusk the willows sway
Like waving arms in a golden glow!
Whisper of trees and a world below
That thrills to a woodland roundelay,
Sweet are the ways when the sun is low,
Fishing time and a drowsy day!

Picture opposite
GRISTMILL
Clinton, New Jersey
Fred Sieb

The Village Blacksmith

Henry Wadsworth Longfellow

Under a spreading chestnut tree,
The village smithy stands;
The smith, a mighty man is he
With large and sinewy hands;
And the muscles of his brawny arms
Are strong as iron bands.

His hair is crisp and black, and long,
His face is like the tan.
His brow is wet with honest sweat;
He earns whate'er he can,
And looks the whole world in the face,
For he owes not any man.

Week in, week out, from morn till night,
You can hear his bellows blow;
You can hear him swing his heavy sledge
With measured beat and slow
Like a sexton ringing the village bell
When the evening sun is low.

And children coming home from school
Look in at the open door;
They love to see the flaming forge,
And hear the bellows roar,
And catch the burning sparks that fly
Like chaff from a thrashing floor.

Thanks, thanks to thee, my worthy friend,
For the lesson thou hast taught!
Thus at the flaming forge of life
Our fortunes must be wrought;
Thus on its sounding anvil shaped
Each burning deed and thought!

He goes on Sunday to the church
And sits among his boys.
He hears the parson pray and preach;
He hears his daughter's voice
Singing in the village choir,
And it makes his heart rejoice.

It sounds to him like her mother's voice
Singing in paradise!
He needs must think of her once more,
How in the grave she lies;
And with his hard, rough hand he wipes
A tear out of his eyes.

Toiling, rejoicing, sorrowing,
Onward through life he goes.
Each morning sees some task begin;
Each evening sees it close;
Something attempted, something done
Has earned a night's repose.

As You Receive Your Diploma

Reginald Holmes

When you step forward to receive
That all-important scroll,
It means you are one step nearer
To your long-awaited goal;

*And yet you'll never say good-bye
To teachers, books, and schools.
Life will give you new assignments,
Harder lessons, stricter rules.*

But you'll find that your diploma
Will open wide the door
Of those golden opportunities
You've been waiting to explore.

*While you gather up your memories
At the end of that long aisle,
You will say good-bye to classmates
With a handclasp and a smile.*

May the knowledge you have gathered
Keep you on the winning side
As you proudly face the future
With confidence and pride.

There are obviously two educations. One should
teach us how to make a living, and the other should
teach us how to live.

James Truslow Adams

Picture opposite
Fred Sieb

Who Has a Hill for a Neighbor

Marion Doyle

Blessed is he
Who has a hill for a neighbor,
Whose privilege any day
May be to climb its skyward sloping
After hours of labor, communing silently—
Outside of time and time's demands—
A precious interlude
Wherein no petty care,
No great desire,
No mediocre matter dare intrude itself
While vision's breadth and depth conspire
A new perspective for the day to come.

All littleness is lost upon a hill.
Here are but harebell, wild geranium,
Deep solitude, and sunlight warm and still—
Such things as make a mirror for the soul,
Enabling one to see life good and whole.

Friendship Road

Dora P. Fortner

Friendship Road is a lovely road,
　　For it's paved with kindly deeds;
Each strip is laid with loving care,
　　With a thought for others' needs.
The shoulders of this road are firm
　　And will bear a heavy load,
And danger signals are not found
　　On the sides of Friendship Road.

Friendship Road is a cheery road
　　As it runs up hill and down
Through the valley of unselfishness
　　To the heights of Friendship Town,
Where friendly folk and kindly folk
　　All peacefully abide,
And friendship's doors all stand ajar
　　To welcome you inside.

Sitting Beside a Lake

Georgia B. Adams

Sitting beside a placid lake
    I lose myself, it seems,
Enjoying haunts of yesterday
    And of tomorrow's dreams.

The water's like a mirror and
    Ripples along the edge;
I reposition my fishing pole
    While sitting on the ledge.

I watch the dragonflies go by
    And see the minnows run;
It's peaceful here beside the lake
    While taking in the sun.

I lose myself in lazy dreams
    While whiling time away;
Sitting beside a placid lake
    Is the way to spend a day!

Picture opposite
SIUSLAU RIVER, OREGON
Monserrate J. Schwartz

The Forest

Rita C. Conley

The forest is calling, and I would go
Far from the city's stress;
Though city-born and city-bred,
My heart's in the wilderness.

I long for the sounds of nature,
The drone of insects in flight,
The crash of a deer through the bushes,
The hoot of an owl at night.

I'd like to sit for hours
Beside a waterfall,
And breathe in the sweet aroma
Of pine trees, straight and tall.

To hear the patter of raindrops
On leaves, instead of on tin,
And the sound of birds sweetly singing
Unmuffled by city's din.

To see the sun rise each morning,
Not o'er the city hall, but a tree,
Yes, I must be off to the woodlands,
For the forest is calling me.

Picture opposite
NEVADA FALLS,
Yosemite National Park, California
George Schwartz

The Old Covered Bridge

D. M. Roads

Old covered bridge of childhood,
Covered with dreams for me,
The road back to you is a long, long road,
But that's where I long to be,
Joyful, carefree and happy,
Dreaming the hours away—
Old covered bridge of childhood
Back in that yesterday.

I'd love to see just once again
Back near the old hometown
This old, old bridge that still is there,
The road a-winding down,
And live again those happy hours
With friends of long ago,
Back near that old hometown of mine,
Back home with folks I know.

Picture opposite
COVERED BRIDGE,
Swiftwater, New Hampshire
Fred Sieb

Rural Scene

Georgia B. Adams

See the cows grazing in silence
   In the hillside pastures sweet;
See the rustic split-rail fences
   Hemming in the fields of wheat.

There's the farmer's boy a'swinging
   On the farmyard swing so high
Or meandering down the footpath
   With his faithful dog so nigh.

See the farmer with his tractor
   Working in the rolling fields;
Visions of the future spur him
   On to what the harvest yields.

And the nestled farmhouse beckons;
   Oh, the whole scene is sublime!
Why don't you walk through the country
   When you have a little time?

I Found Loveliness Today

Carleton Everett Knox

I found loveliness today
Down along life's broad highway,
Saw its beauty in the trees,
Heard it whisper in the breeze,
Listed it in songbird's trill,
Then again in flowing rill,
Felt its warmth in glad sunshine,
Rhythm caught in swaying pine.
All along life's broad highway,
I found loveliness today.

I found loveliness today
Down along life's broad highway,
Beauty in pastures green,
Next in clouds of silvery sheen,
Golden glow at break of day,
Joy in children at their play,
Scented odor of wild rose;
Peace I found where violet grows.
All along life's broad highway,
I found loveliness today.

On the Side Porch

Joellen K. Bland

On the side porch after supper,
We sit in the soft night breeze,
Watching the full moon climb to the barn-top,
Over the tips of the trees,
And perch, golden-proud as a summer peach,
On the weathercock, far beyond our reach.

On the side porch after supper,
We hear the old barn-gate creak.
In the rosehedge, crickets call in time
To the soft, unhurried squeak
Of the old porch swing where I fondle, tease
A kitten or two tumbling on my knees.

On the side porch after chore-time,
My brothers, man-grown, tall,
Hunch on their heels in syringa shadows
Close to the farmhouse wall.
And down on the steps my sisters sing
To music pulled from a banjo's string.

On the side porch after sunset,
The whippoorwills whistle low
From the dusky sweet-gum thicket
To the cool creekland below,
Where under a cloudless August sky
Our rustle-whispering corn rows lie.

We share that time together
When fireflies spark in the eaves;
Soft summer stars twinkle-wink at us
Between the beech tree leaves.
And the field winds carry a kiss of clover,
Here on the side porch when supper's over.

Picture opposite
RURAL GARDEN,
Roxbury, Wisconsin
Ken Dequaine

Overleaf
FERTILE VALLEY,
Marxville, Wisconsin
Ken Dequaine

The Old Home Church

Roy E. Martin

Mid the fond, cherished mem'ries of childhood
   That cling like a beautiful dream,
Come the chimes of a church in the wildwood,
   Near the side of a cool running stream.
When the birds seek their nests, tired of roaming,
   And the dark shadows creep o'er the lea,
Hallowed peace reigns supreme in the gloaming
   While the message they're bringing to me.

Where the fragrance of lilacs and lilies
   Lures the soft sunny breezes along
And the smiles of the daffy-down-dillys
   Greet the notes of the nightingale's song,
While the brook's gentle ripple and bubble
   Reach the shade of the old maple tree,
Far from travail and turmoil and trouble
   Lies the spot that is sacred to me.

The hope that my falt'ring heart foments,
   That urges and carries me on
From the night of my life's darkest moments
   To the glamour and glow of the dawn,
The vision my faith is adorning,
   Be it ever so feeble and frail—
They were shaped there each Sunday morning
   At the little brown church in the vale.

Though the fast-fleeting years bring their treasures,
   Though my dreams' fairy flowers unfold,
The scenes of the sorrows and pleasures
   Of infancy never grow old.
Though I wander in highways and byways
   Or sail o'er the tide and the foam,
An echo from starlighted skyways
   Is calling me—calling me home.

Like the text on the Book's sacred pages,
   Still the chimes as of old seem to say,
"Christ, the light of the world through the ages,
   Is the truth and the life and the way."
At the little brown church in the wildwood
   Whose memory brings joyous tears,
There the lessons were learned in my childhood
   That have guided my feet through the years.

Picture opposite
CENTER SANDWICH,
New Hampshire
Fred Sieb

What's the Use of Poetry?

*Committed to memory, it can be a solace, a joy,
an inspiration—a resource to last a lifetime*

FOR DAYS we had been pressing through the forest of northern Burma to relieve a sister battalion surrounded by the Japanese. As we came out into an open rice field, I looked down the column at the drained, pale faces of the men who would make the assault. I marveled at their courage. Ahead we could hear the artillery. That always brought out the craven in me. But to help give me heart I had in my memory William Ernest Henley's lines about a remnant of the Confederate Army:

> *Rags and tatters, belts and bayonets,*
> *On they swung, the drum a-rolling,*
> *Mum and sour. It looked like fighting,*
> *And they meant it, too, by thunder!*

"Romance," the poem is called, and it begins, "Talk of pluck!" Later, 35 years after World War II, I came upon the text from which I had learned the poem. Yellowed with age, it had been typed by my mother, who sent it to me when I was 14 and working on a farm. She sent me many poems, including another by Henley, which, set to music, is known as "Invictus." It begins:

> *Out of the night that covers me,*
> *Black as the Pit from pole to pole,*
> *I thank whatever gods may be*
> *For my unconquerable soul.*

An unconquerable soul was not a thing that, even at my most euphoric, I could claim. But I was to know times when it took my courage up a notch to recite to myself:

> *Under the bludgeonings of chance,*
> *My head is bloody, but unbowed.*

Hardly written about me! Still ...

I mostly memorized the poems my mother copied for me while riding a hayrake, holding the reins of the chestnut mare, round and round the new-mown field in the timeless hours of summer. I could recognize the truth of Keats's lines:

> *The poetry of earth is never dead;*
> *When all the birds are faint with the hot sun*
> *And hide in cooling trees, a voice will run*
> *From hedge to hedge about the new-mown*
> *mead.*

In this setting, too, I learned of the flower Tennyson held

> *... root and all, in my hand,*
> *Little flower—but if I could understand*
> *What you are, root and all, and all in all,*
> *I should know what God and man is.*

THE ETERNAL, fathomless mystery of creation spoke from these lines. I also read William Blake's declaration that "To see a world in a grain of sand" is to "Hold infinity in the palm of your hand." The truth was so clear I was sure I must have known it all along. Yet without Tennyson and Blake, how long would it have taken me to know I knew it?

In his book *A Study of Poetry,* Bliss Perry, a college professor of mine, wrote of poetry's capacity "for turning fact into truth" and "for lifting the mind, bowed down by wearying

Reprinted with permission from the December 1982 Reader's Digest. Copyright © 1982 by The Reader's Digest Assn., Inc.

thought and haunting fear, into a brooding ecstasy."

Perry wrote, as well, of poetry's capacity "for remolding the broken syllables of human speech into sheer music." That is why, early in life, we are susceptible to the verse of Edgar Allan Poe—because of its music, enhanced by an other-worldly mood:

The skies they were ashen and sober;
The leaves they were crisped and sere—
The leaves they were withering and sere:
It was night, in the lonesome October
Of my most immemorial year;
It was hard by the dim lake of Auber,
In the misty mid region of Weir;
It was down by the dank tarn of Auber,
In the ghoul-haunted woodland of Weir.

Those lines became ineradicable in my memory in college. What much of "Ulalume" meant I could not have said—still cannot. But what did it matter, with mesmerizing lines like "ghoul-haunted woodland of Weir"?

It is only when we memorize poetry that we truly possess it, and it us. My mother spent the last two years of her life bedridden. Her sight had so far left her that she could no longer read. Her hearing soon followed. Now poetry came to her rescue.

In high school Mother had been taught to memorize familiar staples of poetry, and she knew how young Lochinvar came out of the west, what the ancient Mariner told the Wedding Guest and where the wigwam of Nokomis stood (by the shores of Gitchee Gumee). But all roads led her in time to Shakespeare. She could recite his sonnets by the dozen, among them Sonnet XXX, which voices the heartache we all must know toward the end:

When to the sessions of sweet silent thought
I summon up remembrance of things past,
I sigh the lack of many a thing I sought,
And with old woes new wail my dear time's
waste.

ALL OF US, at times every day, are thrown upon our own mental resources and are fortunate if among them are poems we can play over to ourselves. To do this is to know the gratification a musician experiences in performing the work of a master.

If poetry we know by heart can add so to our lives, should memorizing it not have a wider appeal?

Many of us who would enjoy having poetry committed to memory are put off by the seeming effort it requires. We need not be. A habit of reading poetry grows upon one, and there is no need to force ourselves back to well-loved poems. It is not long before we have them half memorized. For my part, I find I soon have the rest if I write the lines on slips of paper I can put in a pocket and take out while waiting at a traffic light, walking, or in an elevator.

Poetry made our own can do wonders for our powers of expression. It can match and intensify our moods, and strengthen our aspirations. Even the poetry of despondency can help us, as Malcolm in Shakespeare's *Macbeth* urges:

Give sorrow words: the grief that does not
speak
Whispers the o'er-fraught heart, and bids
it break.

Great poetry, if we have it in our hearts, can help us—as Kipling enjoins—to

... meet with Triumph and Disaster
And treat those two imposters just the
same.

As Lord Byron puts it in "To Thomas Moore":

Here's a sign to those who love me,
And a smile to those who hate;
And, whatever sky's above me,
Here's a heart for every fate.

Charlton Ogburn

Sunset Song

Brian F. King

There's a time of rich contentment
When the sunset hour is nigh,
When the hush of evening hovers
Where the creeping shadows lie;
It's a time when hearts are tranquil,
When a lonely whippoorwill
Serenades the flaming glory
That adorns the cloud-wreathed hills.

All the world's at rest at sunset
When the sky's a sea of fire,
When men thankfully head homeward
To the things of heart's desire;
It's a time when street lights twinkle
And the stars begin to glow,
Shedding rays of benediction
On the drowsy world below.

There's a special sort of comfort
In the twilight hour's caress,
For it makes each home a castle,
Warm with love and happiness;
And it brings its soothing presence
To the travelers who plod
Roads to hearths that know the blessing
Of the gentle peace of God.

ACKNOWLEDGMENTS

TAPS by Arta Nottingham Chappius and THE STORY OF TAPS by George Daniels. Copyright 1949, THE AMERICAN LEGION MAGAZINE, reprinted by permission. The photo overlooking the Field of Gettysburg used through courtesy of Mrs. Clement J. Carroll. SEASIDE THOUGHTS by Vera Ramsdell Hardman. From HAPPY MOMENTS by Vera Ramsdell Hardman, Copyright © 1972 by Vera Ramsdell Hardman, published by Dorrance & Company. I FOUND LOVELINESS TODAY by Carleton Everett Knox. Used through courtesy of Nona Mae Padgett. RARE FRIEND by James J. Metcalfe. Copyrighted. Courtesy Field Enterprises, Inc. The following by Henry van Dyke: CONTRASTS; FINDING A FRIEND; FRIENDLY TALK; LIFE-GIVING LOVE; A MILE WITH ME; RENDEZVOUS; A SKYLARK SINGING; TIME from THE FRIENDLY YEAR selected by George S. Webster from the works of Henry van Dyke (New York: Charles Scribner's Sons, 1907) Courtesy Charles Scribner's Sons.

Picture Opposite
ANAEHOOMALU BEACH,
Hawaii
Ed Cooper

Discover the Beauty of Summer ...

Welcome the warmth and beauty of summer with the upcoming Countryside issue of Ideals. Travel throughout our majestic nation and view some of the world's most spectacular vistas in brilliant color photographs and outstanding art reproductions. Sweeping rural landscapes and glittering city skylines are yours to explore.

Meander down a quiet country lane ... reminisce about the carefree childhood days of summer in an array of touching poetry and prose selections. Welcome back the showy circus parade and its breathtaking splendor. Celebrate the glorious Fourth of July with author Colleen Reece. Find pleasure in reading "Hiawatha's Childhood" by Henry Wadsworth Longfellow.

Beauty and enjoyment await your discovery—on every page of our tribute to the exciting summer season.

Share all of these enjoyable moments with a special friend or relative by giving a gift subscription to Ideals ... or subscribe yourself and celebrate the wonders of the season in each issue of Ideals.